X

MEL BAY'S

BLUEGRASS BANJO

Edited by
Neil Griffin

By
Sonny
Osborne

Cover photo courtesy of
Liberty Banjo Company,
Bridgeport, Connecticut.

Sonny has been playing the five string banjo since 1950. He is a self-taught musician. He has been working on this method of instruction since 1956, wondering how one person could teach another to play. After many changes, it is now perfected, tried and tested.

Sonny was one of the youngest performers ever to appear on the Grand Ole Opry. He was 13 years old.

FOREWORD

Sonny Osborne has long been one of my favorite banjo players, a real master of the 3-finger bluegrass style and ideas in the full bluegrass solos as well as offering a "from the beginning" approach to the 5-string banjo.

Guitar chords have been added and the STANDARD TABLATURE SYSTEM used by most banjo writers today is used with a few new innovations that make tablature reading easier.

Sonny's banjo method was one of the first to be published in the true Bluegrass Style and will always be a standard. His arrangements are easy to play — whether or not you read music, and his solos are great!
"GOOD PICKIN'."

MEL BAY

BOB OSBORNE — SONNY OSBORNE — BENNY BIRCHFIELD

The Osborne Bros.

The Osborne Brothers began their careers as a team in November, 1953 at radio station WROL in Knoxville, Tennessee. In 1954, they moved to WJR, Detroit, Michigan. From there they went to WWVA in Wheeling, West Virginia (the world's original Jamboree), in October of 1956.

Record-wise, the Osborne Bros. were with MGM Records from April 1956 until August of 1963; and are now under contract to Decca Records. Some of their most popular recordings to date are: "Ruby, Are You Mad"; "Once More"; "She's No Angel" "Fair And Tender Ladies"; "Banjo Boys"; "Lovey Told Me Goodbye"; "Mule Skinner Blues"; "Each Season Changes You"; and their Decca of "Take This Hammer". They also have four great albums: "Country Picking and Hillside Singing"; "Blue Grass Music By The Osbornes"; and "Blue Grass Instrumentals".

On all of their records and stage shows, the Osborne Bros. feature the five string Banjo, Mandolin, and smooth vocal blend, for the best in Blue Grass and Folk Music. The Osbornes have the distinction of being the first Blue Grass group to play a college on the strength of their music alone. This was Antioch College, Yellow Springs, Ohio in early 1959. Their appearance there was such a tremendous success that since then, many other Blue Grass entertainers have been appearing regularly at Colleges all over the country.

THE BANJO

The banjo is an instrument that cannot be mastered overnight. As in all instruments, it takes long hours and deep concentration to play correctly.

Read the instructions carefully. Go slowly and learn each part thoroughly as you go. Practice when you can devote your full time and attention to the banjo. Be fair to yourself — It is easier to remember what you learn right, than to forget what you learn wrong.

I will make a suggestion here. If you have difficulty when learning the tunes, in concentrating on both hands at once, try learning the right hand first and then add the noting of the left hand.

This works well for some people, and for others it is best to put both hands together from the start.

HOLDING THE BANJO

TONE

One of the most important things you will ever want to learn is how to control the tone of your banjo playing. This is where I have heard many people falter badly.

You must find the playing position for your right hand which will produce the best tones. Begin by placing the hand near the bridge. While moving your fingers in a forward roll (thumb, index, middle, thumb, index, middle, etc.) move your hand forward toward the neck of the banjo. Notice the change in tone. Moving the hand back and forth in this manner, you will be able to judge where your hand should be placed to get the best tone. When you have found what you consider to be the best playing position, make it a habit to play at this exact position at all times. (Make two very light pencil marks on the head, at the points where the ring and little finger rest on the head. This may help you get used to finding your position automatically.)

Always be sure the metal finger picks strike the strings flat and solid. They should hit the string in the middle of the pick. If your picks have holes, they should strike the strings from the hole directly out the middle to the end of the pick.

The picks must hit the strings correctly for a clear, solid tone.

THE LEFT HAND

The left hand, or noting hand, should move freely, keeping all fingers loose and comfortable.

In answer to the common question of which fingers to use — use the finger closest to the note so that the other fingers are free for fast action.

Use all fingers as equally as is practical. It looks much better and it helps produce clear, clean notes.

THE RIGHT HAND

RIGHT HAND POSITION

The right hand is by far the most important thing in playing Banjo, Bluegrass Style.

The ring finger and little finger are placed in a stationary position, near the bridge, and should remain in this position at all times. The wrist should be bent to give maximum power in your roll.

The hand should be placed in a comfortable position while playing. Yet, it is also important to your playing to have it in the best position to obtain the best tone from your instrument.

RIGHT HAND FINGERING

The middle finger (designated in the tunes by - M) is always used **only** on the first string.

The index finger (designated by - I) is used on the second and third strings.

The thumb (designated by - T) is used on the second, third, fourth and fifth strings.

SL - is used to indicate a Slide.
H - is used to indicate a Hammer.
P - is used to indicate a Pull-off.

PICKS

For best tone quality, I suggest metal picks for the index and middle fingers and a plastic thumb pick. These can be purchased at any music store where parts or supplies for instruments are sold.

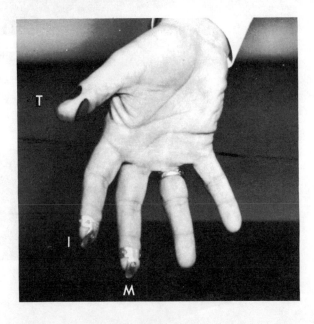

BRIDGE

The 'ring' or sound of a banjo can be altered in several ways.

If the sound is too deep or coarse, use a higher bridge. Also, tighten the head until it is firm.

You can also thin that part of the bridge where the strings cross over it. Use a very fine file or light sandpaper. The thinner the bridge, the brighter the sound.

When you have your banjo set up to give its best tone, consistently and to your satisfaction — it's a good idea not to allow many people to play it or work on it. Everyone has his own idea on how a banjo should sound, and a fairly strong "Hands off" policy can save you a lot of trouble.

ADJUSTING THE BRIDGE

If ever your banjo does not note true from the 12th to the 22nd fret, you can correct this by adjusting the bridge.

If the banjo notes flat, move the bridge forward, toward the neck to the desired position.
If the banjo notes sharp, move the bridge back toward the tail piece.

STRINGS

To get maximum volume and the best tone from your banjo, I suggest very light gauge strings. They are easier to note and seem to hold a good tone longer, for this style of playing.

The 1st, 2nd, 3rd and 5th strings should be plain steel (no wrapping). The 4th string should be wound or wrapped.

A good set of strings should last a month to six weeks without losing too much tone. A lot of people change and replace strings before they are actually worn out.
To preserve strings, wipe them clean after playing.

TUNING THE BANJO

G - BLUEGRASS

The 5 strings are tuned to a piano as shown.

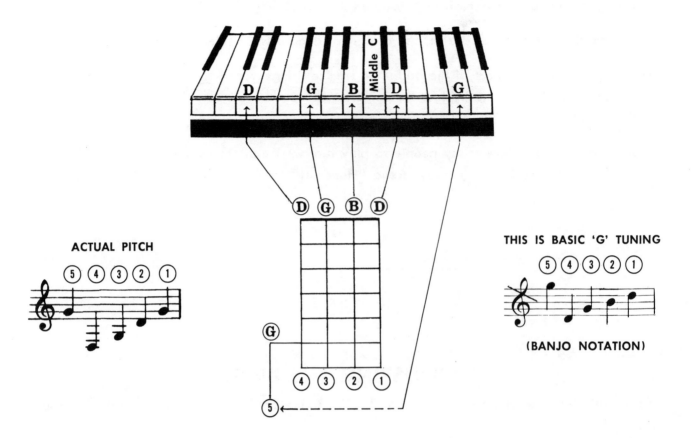

ACTUAL PITCH

THIS IS BASIC 'G' TUNING

(BANJO NOTATION)

Banjo music written an octave higher than the actual sound, will be indicated by

When the music is written exactly as heard, it will be indicated by

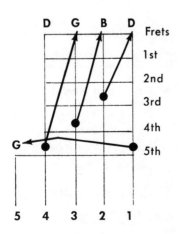

← ANOTHER WAY TO TUNE

Tune the first string to 'D' (Next above middle C).

Tune 2nd string, noted at 3rd fret, to same pitch as open first string.

Tune 3rd string, noted at 4th fret, to same pitch as open second string.

Tune the 5th string to sound the same as the 1st string noted at the 5th fret.

'D' TUNING

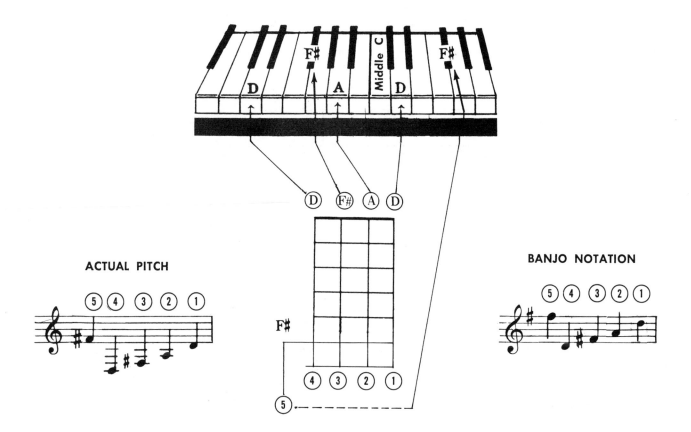

ACTUAL PITCH

BANJO NOTATION

In 'D' tuning, a banjo may be played with the same basic rolls as in normal 'G' tuning.

Although there are no solos in this book for the "D" tuning, it is important to know as there are many Blue Grass numbers in "D".

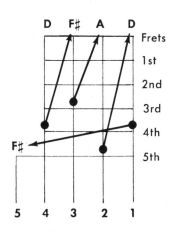

← ANOTHER WAY TO TUNE

Tune 1st string to D (next above middle C).

Tune 2nd string, noted 5th fret, to same pitch as open first string.

Tune 3rd string, noted at 3rd fret, to same pitch as open 2nd string.

Tune 4th string, noted at 4th, to same pitch as open 3rd string.

Tune the 5th string to same pitch as the 1st string noted at the 4th fret.

THE RUDIMENTS OF MUSIC
The Staff

Music is written on a STAFF consisting of FIVE LINES and FOUR SPACES.

The lines and spaces are numbered upward as shown:

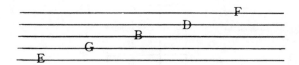

They also have LETTER names.

The LINES are named as follows: 1 - E, 2 - G, 3 - B, 4 - D, 5 - F.

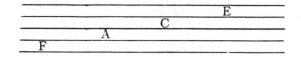

The letters can easily be remembered by the sentence —

Every Good Boy Does Fine.

The letter-names of the SPACES are: 1 - F, 2 - A, 3 - C, 4 - E.

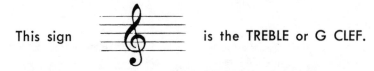

They spell the word **F-A-C-E.**

The musical alphabet has seven letters — A, B, C, D, E, F, G.

The Clef

This sign 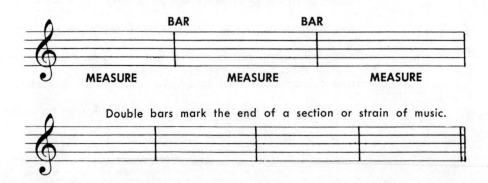 is the TREBLE or G CLEF.

All Banjo music will be written in this clef.

The STAFF is divided into MEASURES by vertical lines called BARS.

Double bars mark the end of a section or strain of music.

NOTES

This is a NOTE:

A note has three parts.

They are — the HEAD ● , the STEM | , and the FLAG ♪ .

Notes may be placed in the staff,

above the staff,

and

below the staff.

A note will bear the name of the line or space it occupies on the staff.

The location of a note in, above or below the staff will indicate the Pitch.

PITCH: the highness or lowness of a tone.

TONE: a musical sound.

The SHAPE of a note will indicate the LENGTH of its sound.

This is a **WHOLE NOTE** 𝗈 The head is hollow. It does not have a stem.	This is a **HALF NOTE** ♩ The head is hollow. It has a stem.
This is a **QUARTER NOTE** ♩ The head is solid. It has a stem.	This is an **EIGHTH NOTE** ♪ The head is solid. It has a stem and a flag.

RESTS

A REST is a sign used to designate a period of silence.

This period of silence will be of the same duration of time as the note to which it corresponds.

This is a **WHOLE REST.** ▬ Note that it hangs DOWN from the line.	This is a **HALF REST** ▬ Note that it lays ON the line.
This is a **QUARTER REST** 𝄽	This is an **EIGHTH REST** 𝄾

Notes and Comparative Rests

NOTES	Whole 4 counts	Half 2 counts	Quarter 1 count	Eighth 2 for 1 count
RESTS	▬	▬	𝄽	𝄾

Time Signatures

At the beginning of every piece of music is placed a time signature. The top figure indicates the number of counts per measure. The bottom figure indicates the type of note that receives one count. If the lower number is a 4, a quarter note (♩) has been chosen to represent one count. We will learn later how figures other than 4 are sometimes used as the lower number.

Three examples of time signatures

A large C thus:  signifies so called "common time" and is simply another way of designating 4/4 time.

The Rule of the Dot

A dot placed after a note or a rest increases its time value by one half.

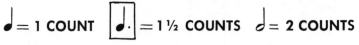

EXAMPLES ♩ = 1 COUNT ♩. = 1½ COUNTS ♩ = 2 COUNTS ♩. = 3 COUNTS

Note Review

A Note has _____ parts.

They are the_____ the_____ and the_____

Notes may be placed _____ the staff.

Notes may be placed _____ the staff.

Notes may be placed _____ the staff.

A Note will bear the Name of the _____

or _____ it occupies.

_____ The Height or Depth of a Tone.

_____ A Musical Sound.

The _____ of a Note will indicate

the _____ of its Sound.

A Whole Note has a _____

The _____ is hollow.

It does not have a _____

A Half Note has two parts. They are the

_____ and _____ . The Head is _____

A Quarter Note has two parts. They are the

_____ and _____ The Head is _____

An Eighth Note has three parts.

They are the _____ , the _____

and the _____ The head is _____

A _____ is a sign of _____

This period of _____ will be of the same _____

of _____ as the _____ to which it corresponds.

A Whole Rest hangs _____ from the line.

A Half Rest _____ the line.

Draw Three Quarter Rests. _____

Draw Three Eighth Rests. _____

Notes on the First String (D)

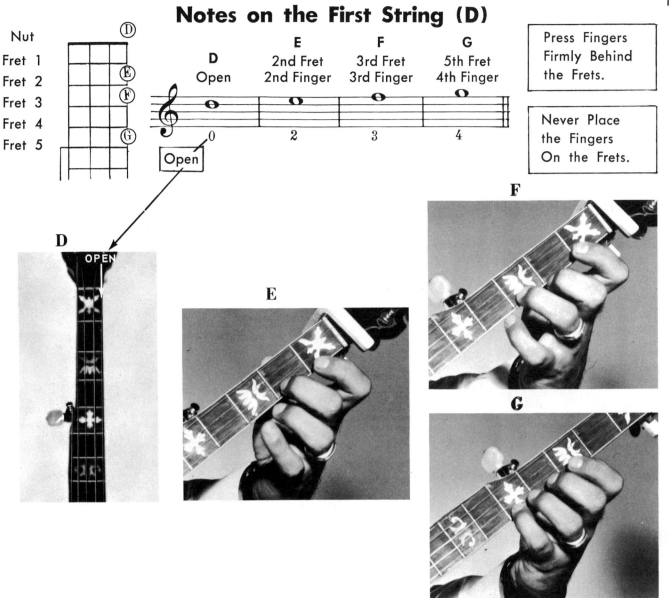

Press Fingers Firmly Behind the Frets.

Never Place the Fingers On the Frets.

Notes on the Second String (B)

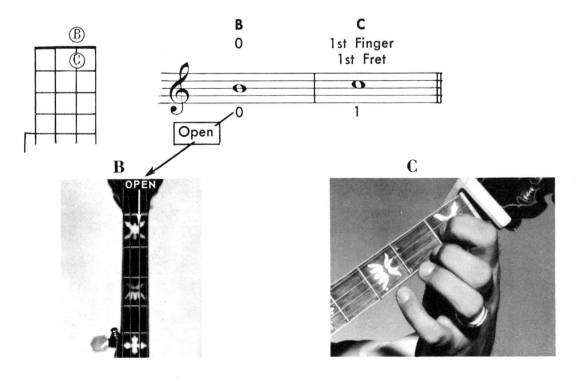

Notes on the Third String (G)

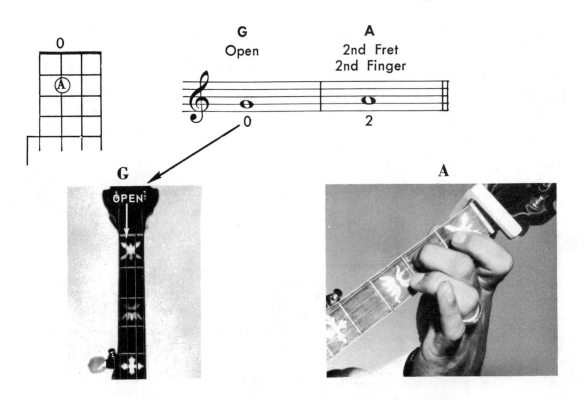

G	A
Open	2nd Fret
	2nd Finger

G

A

Notes on the Fourth String (D)

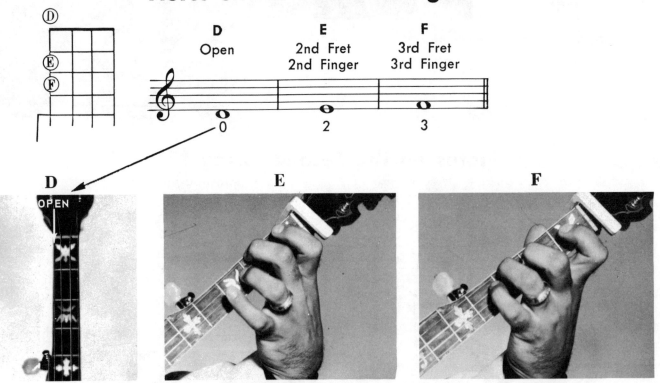

D	E	F
Open	2nd Fret	3rd Fret
	2nd Finger	3rd Finger

D

E

F

The Fifth String (G)

The open 5th string sounds high G ━━━━━━━━ This is the same musical pitch as the 1st string, 5th fret. For convenience in fingering, both of these are used. (always refer to the tablature when in doubt as to which "g" to use.)

TABLATURE

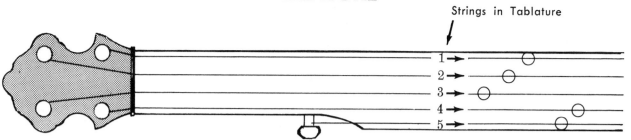

Strings in Tablature

Tablature is simply a drawing of the 5 strings of the banjo with numbers showing you to either pick a string open or in which fret to press a string down to produce the note called for in the music.

This tablature will appear throughout this book directly under each note of music showing which string and in which fret every note is found on the banjo.

Shown below are examples of tablature with an explanation of each item.

1 ————————————— 1st string
2 ————————————— 2nd string
3 ————————————— 3rd string
4 ————————————— 4th string
5 ————————————— 5th string

There are five lines in the tablature, one for each string on the banjo as shown above.

The numbers placed on the tablature lines show in which fret to press down the left hand fingers.

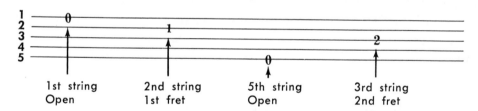

| 1st string | 2nd string | 5th string | 3rd string |
| Open | 1st fret | Open | 2nd fret |

When 2 or more notes are played at the same time the numbers are above one another as shown below.

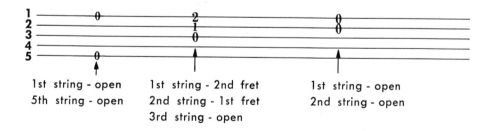

1st string - open   1st string - 2nd fret   1st string - open
5th string - open   2nd string - 1st fret   2nd string - open
                  3rd string - open

FOR ADDITIONAL STUDY MATERIAL AND SOLOS
SEE MEL BAY'S

Complete Bluegrass Banjo Method – by Neil Griffin
Splitting the Licks – by Janet Davis
Back-Up Banjo – by Janet Davis
Deluxe Encyclopedia of Banjo Chords
Complete Banjo Book – by Neil Griffin

TABLATURE SYMBOLS

The symbols used in this book are very important in learning to play. Be sure to learn and memorize each one and know exactly what it means before trying to play.

Below, in detail, are the symbols and their meanings. Study them carefully.

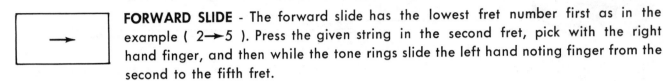

FORWARD SLIDE - The forward slide has the lowest fret number first as in the example (2→5). Press the given string in the second fret, pick with the right hand finger, and then while the tone rings slide the left hand noting finger from the second to the fifth fret.

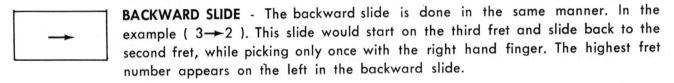

BACKWARD SLIDE - The backward slide is done in the same manner. In the example (3→2). This slide would start on the third fret and slide back to the second fret, while picking only once with the right hand finger. The highest fret number appears on the left in the backward slide.

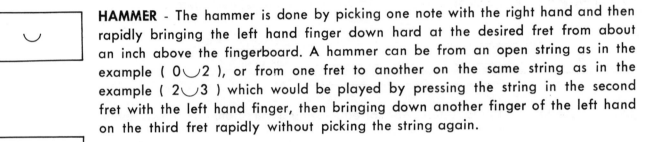

HAMMER - The hammer is done by picking one note with the right hand and then rapidly bringing the left hand finger down hard at the desired fret from about an inch above the fingerboard. A hammer can be from an open string as in the example (0‿2), or from one fret to another on the same string as in the example (2‿3) which would be played by pressing the string in the second fret with the left hand finger, then bringing down another finger of the left hand on the third fret rapidly without picking the string again.

CHIME - Special instructions are given on page 27.

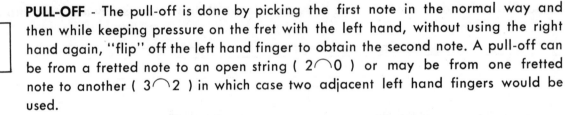

PULL-OFF - The pull-off is done by picking the first note in the normal way and then while keeping pressure on the fret with the left hand, without using the right hand again, "flip" off the left hand finger to obtain the second note. A pull-off can be from a fretted note to an open string (2⌢0) or may be from one fretted note to another (3⌢2) in which case two adjacent left hand fingers would be used.

COUNTING TIME IN TABLATURE

Counting time in tablature will be exactly the same as in regular musical notation, using a time signature at the beginning, with measures separated by bar lines, and with stems being used for the different time values.

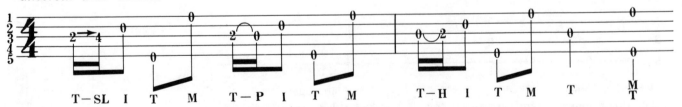

The only difference in tablature counting will be that if a note is to be held longer than one count it will be shown as follows.

The first count will have the regular quarter note stem and will be connected to one additional quarter note stem for each additional count the note is to be held.

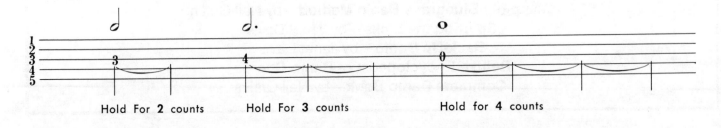

Hold For **2** counts   Hold For **3** counts   Hold for **4** counts

PREPARATORY SONGS

London Bridge

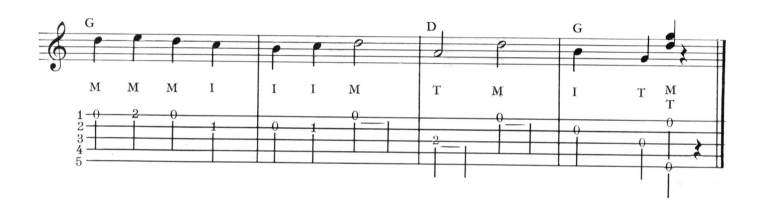

Yankee Doodle

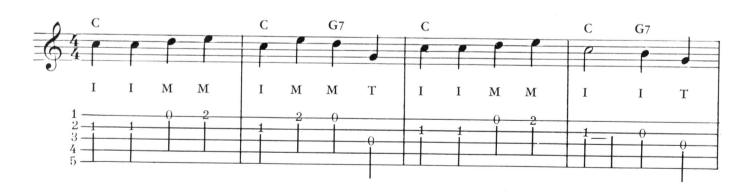

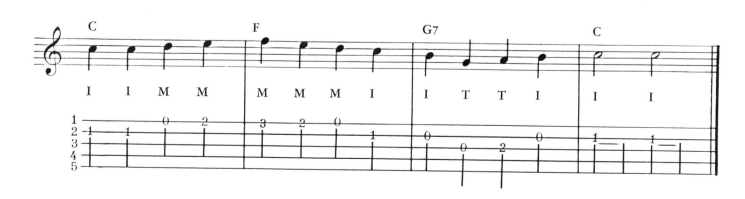

Go Tell Aunt Rhody

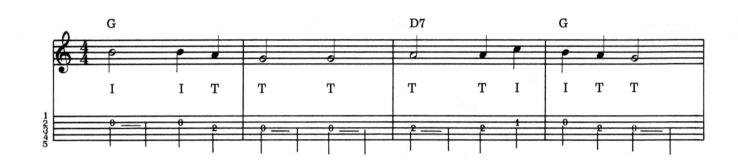

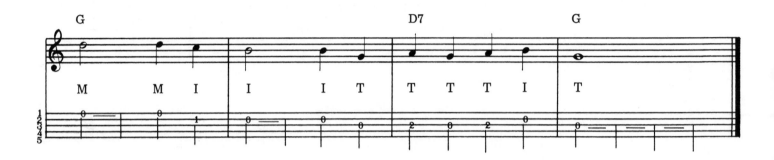

Little Brown Jug

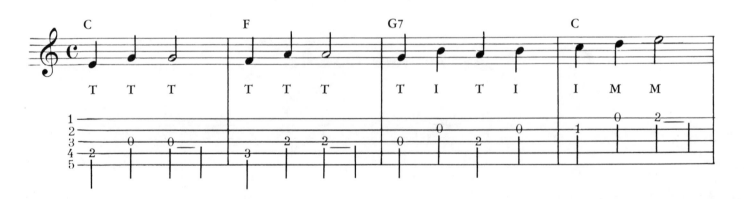

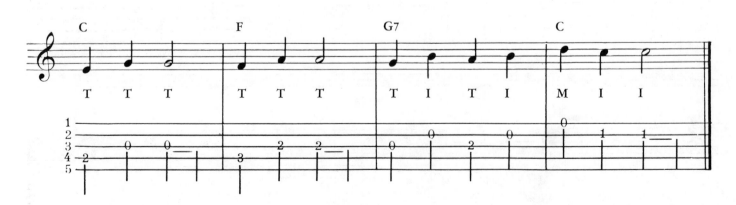

Dots before and after a double bar mean to repeat the measures between.

Cripple Creek

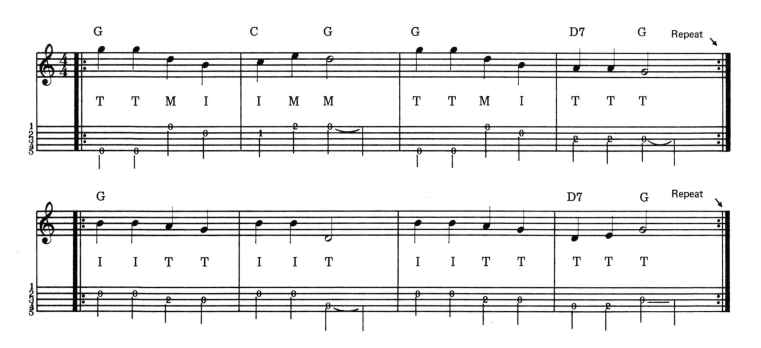

Shady Grove

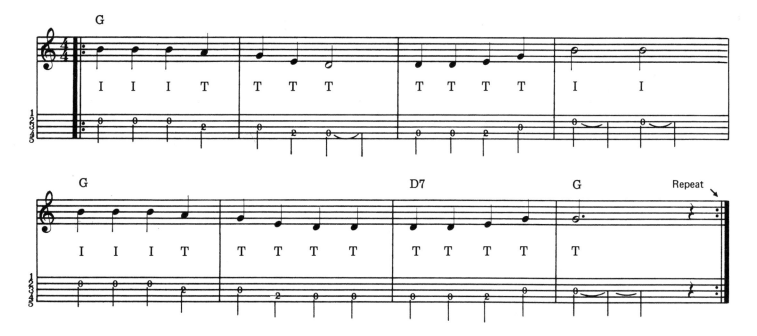

The Tie

The Tie is a curved line between two notes of the same pitch or staff location.

The first note is played and held for the time duration of both notes.

The second note is not played but held.

Examples

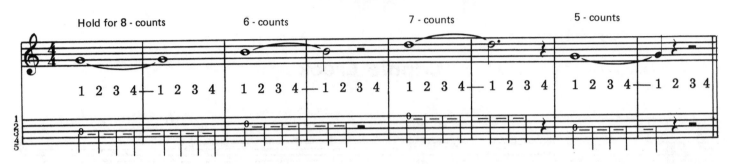

Pick-up Notes

One or more notes at the beginning of a strain before the first measure are referred to as pick-up notes.

The rhythm for pick-up notes is taken from the last measure of the selection and the beats are counted as such. (Note the two beats in the last measure.)

Red River Valley

The Eighth Note

An eighth note receives one-half beat (One quarter note equals two eighth notes).

An eighth note will have a head, stem, and flag. If two or more are in successive order they may be connected by a bar (See Example).

Eighth Notes and Eighth Rests

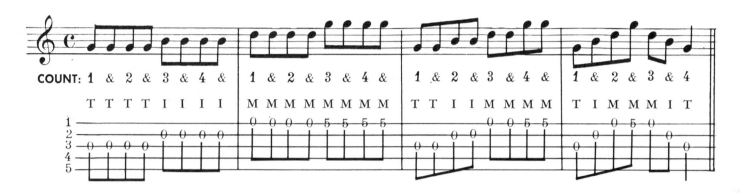

I've Been Working on the Railroad

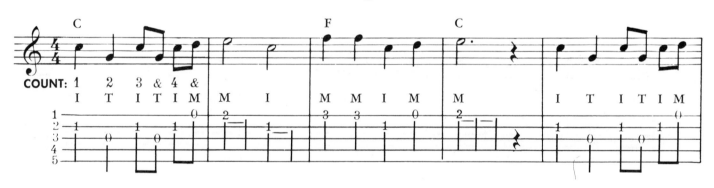

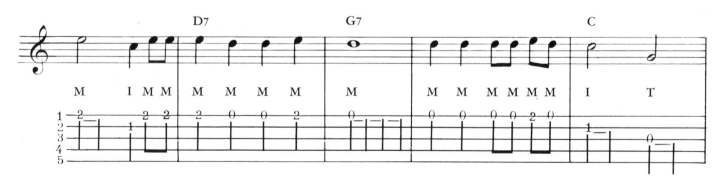

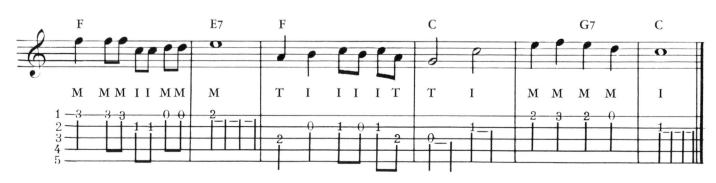

Tom Dooley

It A'int Gonna Rain No More

The Sharp

The Sharp (♯) placed before a note raises the sound of that note one fret.

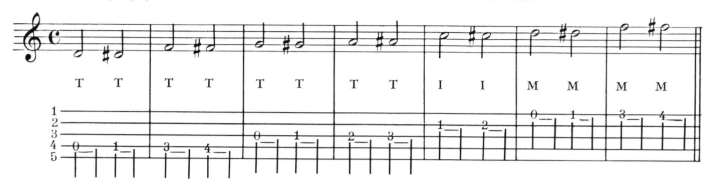

The Sharpie

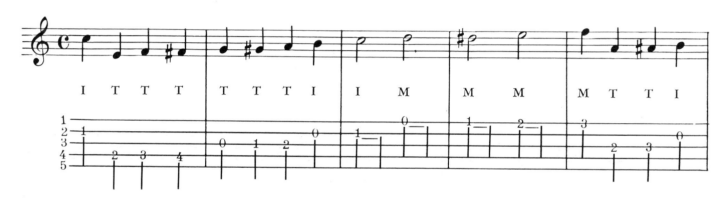

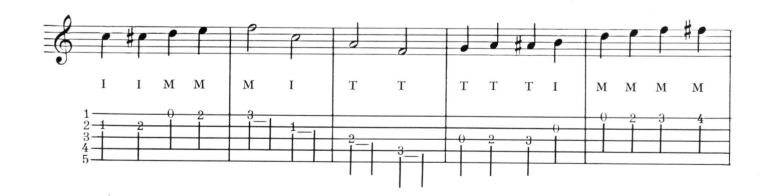

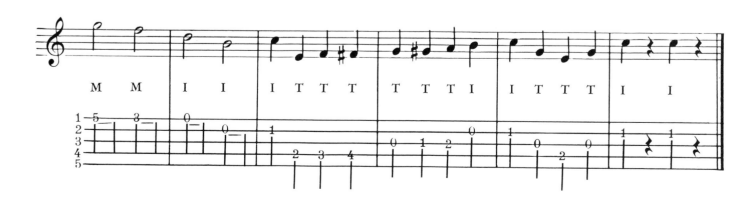

The Flat

♭

A Flat (♭) placed before a note lowers the sound of that note one fret.

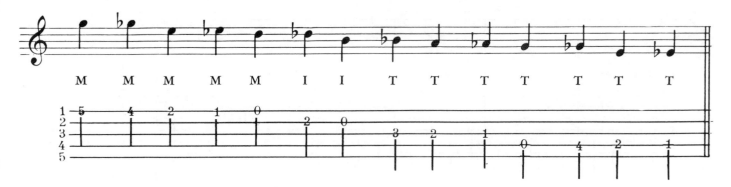

Flat Land

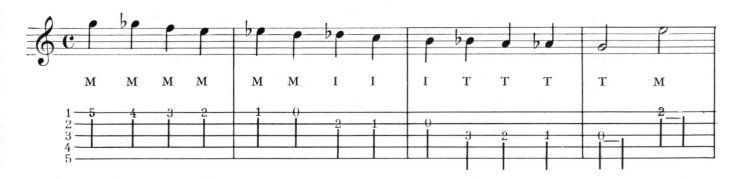

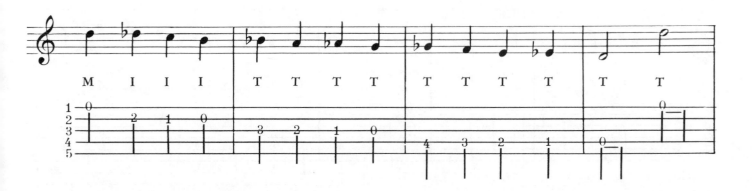

The Natural

A Natural (♮) placed before a note restores that note to its natural or regular position.

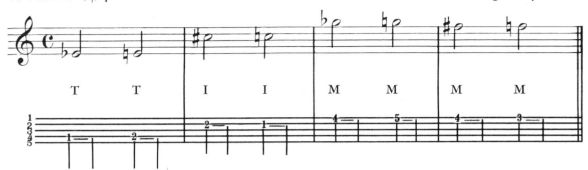

A Pair of Naturals

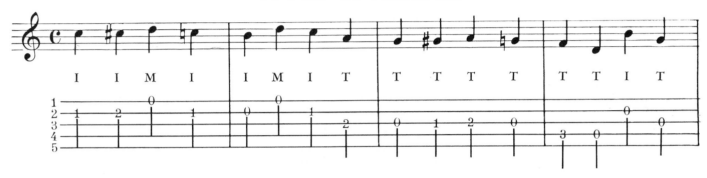

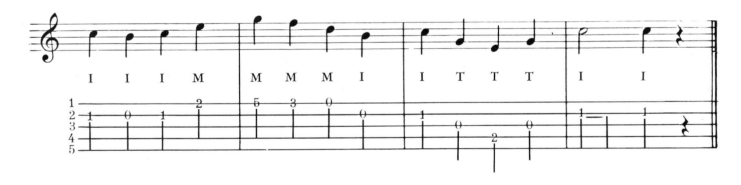

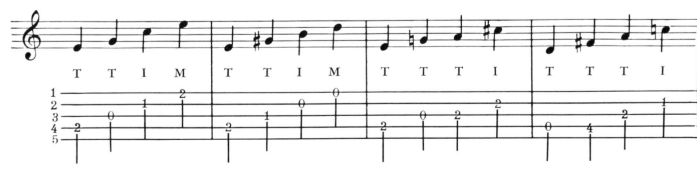

The Key of G

The Key of G will have one Sharp. It will be identified by this signature:

The F-notes will be played as shown.

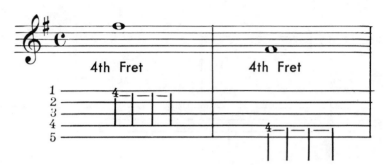

Gee-Whiz

THE CAPO

A capo is used to clamp the first four strings down in order to play in different keys. This saves re-tuning of the first four strings.

The fifth, or short string must be tuned up the same number of frets as the placement of the capo. Example: Capo placed at 4th — tune the 5th string 4 frets higher.

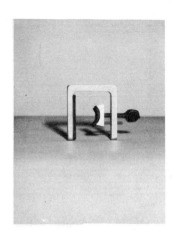

CHIMES

A banjo can be chimed in four places on the standard fingerboard. These are the 5th, 7th, 12th and 19th frets. The chimes on the 5th and 12th frets are in the key of G. The chimes on the 7th and 19th frets are in the key of D.

To chime — place the 3rd finger of the left hand, **lightly, across all five** strings at the desired fret. Barely touch the strings. When placed correctly, you can feel a string vibrate under your finger as it is picked with the right hand.

Chimes are not used very often. A tune which does use them is included in this book, "Sonny's Chimes." The chimes will be indicated by the symbol — ⓧ.

ROLLS

A **forward** roll is when the designated strings are played in a forward rotation — thumb, index, middle, — thumb, index, middle.

A **backward** roll would be the opposite — middle, index, thumb, — middle, index, thumb.

A **split** roll is a combination of parts or all or backward and forward rolls — thumb, index, middle (forward) thumb, middle index (backward) put together.

An **Alternating** roll is — thumb, index, thumb, middle — thumb, index, thumb, middle.

Learn the exercises thoroughly before beginning the tunes. These will accustom your fingers to moving smoothly and accurately. It will take practice, I assure you.

The roll is the basis of all bluegrass banjo picking and you should practice all of the patterns shown over and over until you can play them smoothly, clearly, and with good speed. Start slowly and then steadily build up your speed being quite sure that all the notes of the rolls are still clear as you get faster. In the following exercises you will learn the rolls first and then how to slide, hammer, and pull-off within the roll patterns. **Study this section very carefully before trying to play the solos.**

Forward Roll Patterns

Backward Roll Patterns

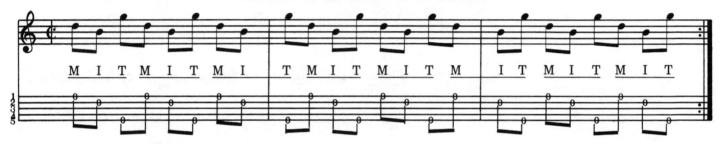

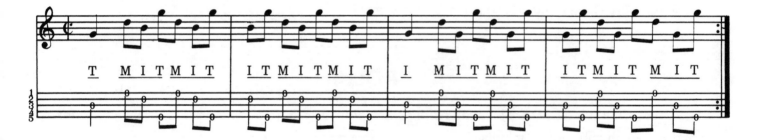

Split Roll Patterns

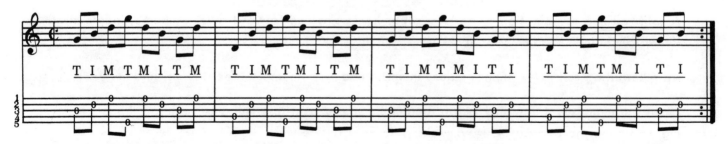

Alternating Roll Patterns

Slides

Hammers

Pull-offs

Backward Slides   Double-Hammers

Basic Bluegrass Sound

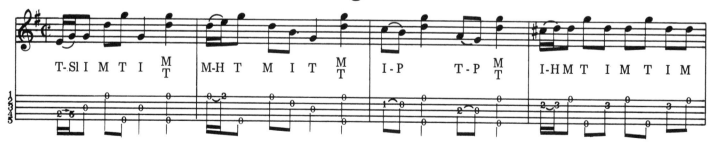

— BLUEGRASS SOLOS —
Sonny's Breakdown

Old Joe Clark

Sonny's Chimes

Chimes — 8va (sounds an octave higher)

Red Wing

36

Cumberland Echoes

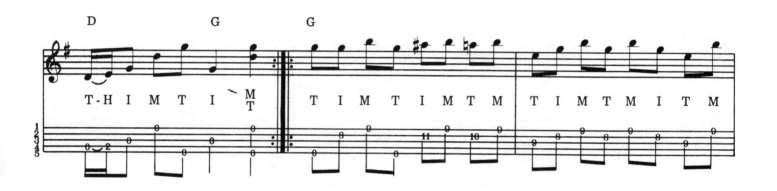

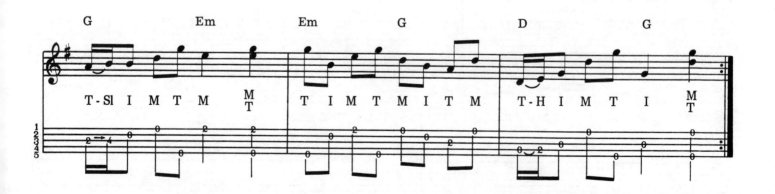

John Henry

The Bird

THE BLUE GRASS STYLE CHORDS
THE MAJOR CHORDS

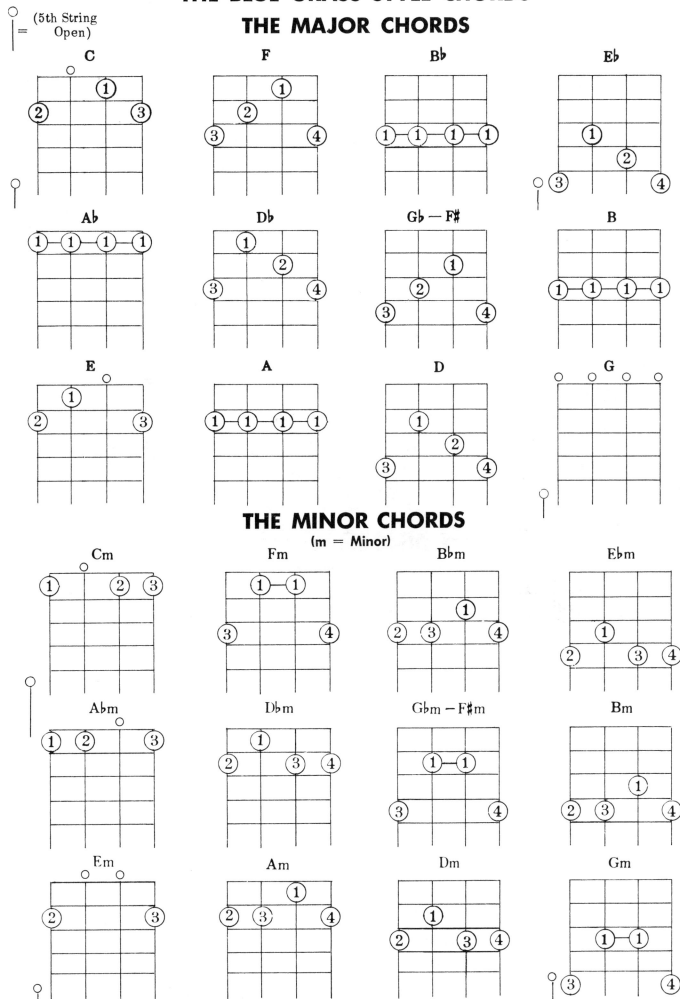

THE MINOR CHORDS
(m = Minor)

THE SEVENTH CHORDS

(7 = Seventh Chord)

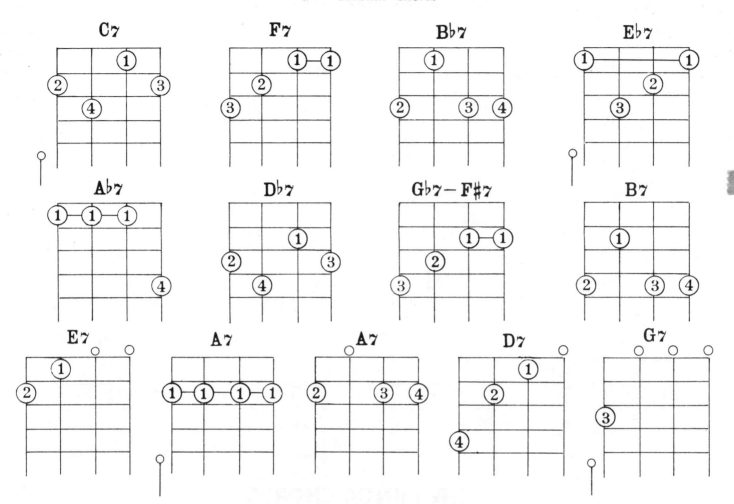

C7 F7 Bb7 Eb7

Ab7 Db7 Gb7 – F#7 B7

E7 A7 A7 D7 G7

THE DIMINISHED CHORDS

(−) = Diminished

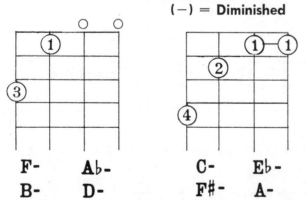
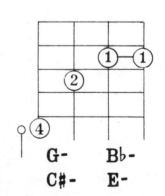

F- Ab- C- Eb- G- Bb-
B- D- F#- A- C#- E-

THE AUGMENTED CHORDS

(+) = Augmented

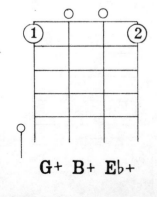
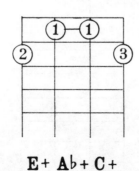
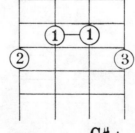
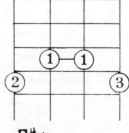

G+ B+ Eb+ E+ Ab+ C+ F+ A+ C#+ / Db+ F#+ / Gb+ Bb+ D+